Ecosystems
Deserts

Erinn Banting

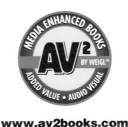

www.av2books.com

MEDIA ENHANCED BOOKS
AV²
BY WEIGL™
ADDED VALUE • AUDIO VISUAL

Go to **www.av2books.com**, and enter this book's unique code.

BOOK CODE

D 8 6 2 4 4

AV² by Weigl brings you media enhanced books that support active learning.

AV² provides enriched content that supplements and complements this book. Weigl's AV² books strive to create inspired learning and engage young minds in a total learning experience.

Your AV² Media Enhanced books come alive with...

Audio
Listen to sections of the book read aloud.

Key Words
Study vocabulary, and complete a matching word activity.

Video
Watch informative video clips.

Quizzes
Test your knowledge.

Embedded Weblinks
Gain additional information for research.

Slide Show
View images and captions, and prepare a presentation.

Try This!
Complete activities and hands-on experiments.

... and much, much more!

Published by AV² by Weigl
350 5th Avenue, 59th Floor
New York, NY 10118
Website: www.av2books.com   www.weigl.com

Library of Congress Cataloging-in-Publication Data

Banting, Erinn.
   Deserts / Erinn Banting.
      p. cm. -- (Ecosystems)
   Includes index.
   ISBN 978-1-61690-644-3 (hardcover : alk. paper) -- ISBN 978-1-61690-650-4 (softcover : alk. paper)
   1. Desert ecology--Juvenile literature. I. Title.
   QH541.5.D4B366 2011
   577.54--dc22

                          2010050988

Printed in the United States of America in North Mankato, Minnesota
1 2 3 4 5 6 7 8 9 15 14 13 12 11

052011
WEP37500

Project Coordinator Aaron Carr
Design Sonja Vogel

Every reasonable effort has been made to trace ownership and to obtain permission to reprint copyright material. The publishers would be pleased to have any errors or omissions brought to their attention so that they may be corrected in subsequent printings.

Photo Credits
Weigl acknowledges Getty Images as its primary photo supplier for this title.

Contents

What is a Desert Ecosystem?

Most desert plants grow close to the ground because of intense heat and lack of water.

Earth is home to millions of different **organisms**, all of which have specific survival needs. These organisms rely on their environment, or the place where they live, for their survival. All plants and animals have relationships with their environment. They interact with the environment itself, as well as the other plants and animals within the environment. These interactions create **ecosystems**.

Deserts are a type of ecosystem. Most deserts are barren landscapes dotted with massive rock structures or sand dunes. Some of the hottest and driest places on Earth are deserts. Very little rain falls in deserts, and the temperatures are often very hot. In any desert, it is difficult for plants and animals to survive.

Deserts are home to some of the most unique creatures in the world. Many **species** have **adapted** to these harsh living conditions and a lack of food and water.

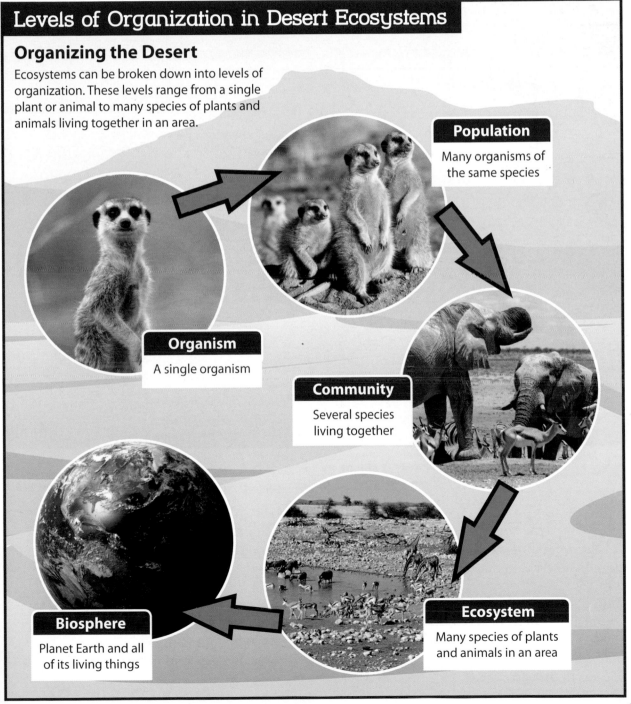

Levels of Organization in Desert Ecosystems

Organizing the Desert

Ecosystems can be broken down into levels of organization. These levels range from a single plant or animal to many species of plants and animals living together in an area.

Population
Many organisms of the same species

Organism
A single organism

Community
Several species living together

Ecosystem
Many species of plants and animals in an area

Biosphere
Planet Earth and all of its living things

Where in the World?

The Sahara Desert of Africa is the world's largest desert ecosystem. Although more than 90 percent of the desert is not suited to support life, it is home to about 500 plant species.

Many of the largest deserts in the world are located directly north and south of the **equator**, near the **Tropic of Cancer** and the **Tropic of Capricorn**. The closer a desert is to the equator, the hotter its temperatures.

The Sahara Desert is 3.3 million square miles (8.6 million square kilometers) and covers nearly one-third of northern Africa. Neighboring the Sahara is the Arabian Desert. This desert is located in Egypt. It covers about 900,000 square miles (2.3 million sq. km) from the Nile River Valley in the west to the Red Sea and the Gulf of Suez in the east.

Australia is home to the Great Victoria Desert, which measures 163,900 square miles (424,400 sq. km). It is one of four deserts in Australia's interior. These four deserts are part of a region called the Outback.

The North American Desert, located in the southeastern United States, includes the Great Basin, Mojave, Sonora, and Chihuahuan Deserts. The estimated size of this desert varies from 500,000 to 730,000 square miles (3.2 million to 4.7 million sq. km).

The Gobi Desert is the largest desert in Asia. It stretches about 500,000 square miles (1.3 million sq. km) through China and Mongolia.

Eco Facts

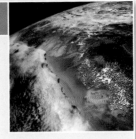

Though the size of Earth's deserts is always changing, they cover about 33 percent of Earth's land surface. That is about 8.6 million square miles (22 million sq. km). Some deserts flood, but they still do not receive enough rain to fill and sustain a river. Water either seeps into underground rivers beneath the soil, or it evaporates.

The arctic regions of the North and South Poles are home to polar, or cold, deserts. These deserts have freezing temperatures throughout the entire year.

Mapping the Deserts

Desert ecosystems are found on most of the world's continents. This map shows where the world's major deserts are located. Find the place where you live on the map. Do you live close to a desert? If not, which deserts are closest to you?

Legend

■ Desert

□ Ocean

∿ River

Scale at Equator

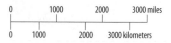

0   1000   2000   3000 miles

0   1000   2000   3000 kilometers

N

ARCTIC OCEAN

NORTH PACIFIC OCEAN

NORTH AMERICA

Great Basin Desert, United States

Mojave Desert, United States

NORTH ATLANTIC OCEAN

Chihuahuan Desert, United States and Mexico

EQUATOR

SOUTH PACIFIC OCEAN

Sechura Desert, Peru

SOUTH AMERICA

Atacama Desert, Peru and Chile

Sonoran Desert

Location: North America (United States and Mexico)
Size: 120,000 square miles (310,800 sq. km)
Fact: The Sonoran Desert is the wettest desert in the world. It receives up to 15 inches (380 millimeters) of rain each year. Most of this rain falls during the monsoon, or rainy, season, between July and September.

Patagonian Desert

Location: South America (Argentina and Chile)
Size: 260,000 square miles (673,000 sq. km)
Fact: The Patagonian is the largest desert in the Americas. Temperatures in this desert range from 12° Fahrenheit (−11° Celsius) to 113° F (45° C).

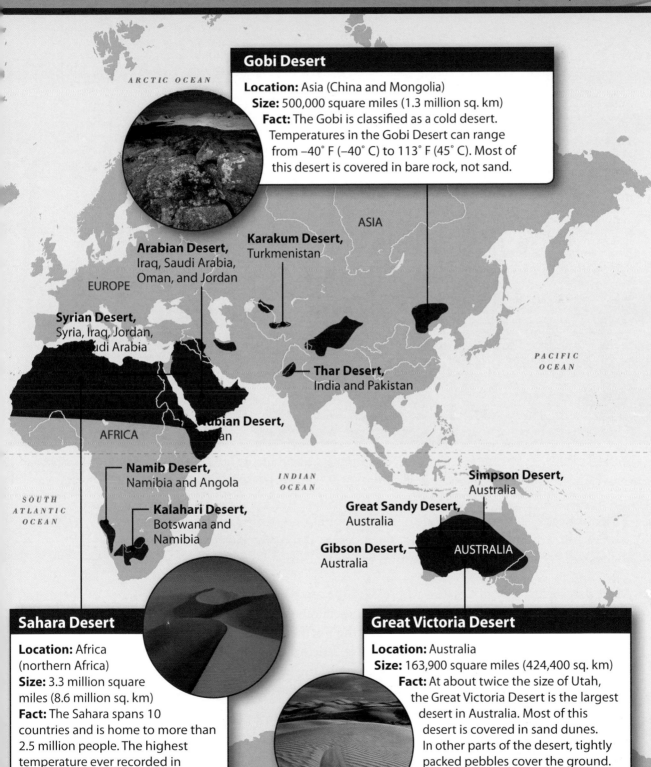

ARCTIC OCEAN

Gobi Desert

Location: Asia (China and Mongolia)
Size: 500,000 square miles (1.3 million sq. km)
Fact: The Gobi is classified as a cold desert. Temperatures in the Gobi Desert can range from −40° F (−40° C) to 113° F (45° C). Most of this desert is covered in bare rock, not sand.

ASIA

Arabian Desert, Iraq, Saudi Arabia, Oman, and Jordan

Karakum Desert, Turkmenistan

EUROPE

Syrian Desert, Syria, Iraq, Jordan, ...udi Arabia

PACIFIC OCEAN

Thar Desert, India and Pakistan

...bian Desert, ...an

AFRICA

Namib Desert, Namibia and Angola

INDIAN OCEAN

Simpson Desert, Australia

SOUTH ATLANTIC OCEAN

Kalahari Desert, Botswana and Namibia

Great Sandy Desert, Australia

Gibson Desert, Australia

AUSTRALIA

Sahara Desert

Location: Africa (northern Africa)
Size: 3.3 million square miles (8.6 million sq. km)
Fact: The Sahara spans 10 countries and is home to more than 2.5 million people. The highest temperature ever recorded in the Sahara was 136° F (58° C).

Great Victoria Desert

Location: Australia
Size: 163,900 square miles (424,400 sq. km)
Fact: At about twice the size of Utah, the Great Victoria Desert is the largest desert in Australia. Most of this desert is covered in sand dunes. In other parts of the desert, tightly packed pebbles cover the ground.

ANTARCTICA

Desert Climates

Winter precipitation in the desert usually falls as rain. When temperatures are low enough, however, precipitation sometimes falls as snow.

Desert ecosystems receive little or no precipitation. Precipitation is rain, snow, or fog. For an area to be considered a desert, it must receive fewer than 10 inches (25 centimeters) of precipitation each year.

Most deserts are very hot places, where daytime temperatures can reach 140° F (60° C). Sand and hot sunshine are often associated with deserts, but not all deserts are warm. There are cold deserts at the north and south poles. Cold deserts are covered with ice or snow. There is little precipitation in these deserts, but the temperature is so cold the snow does not melt. Over time, tall layers of snow and ice form. Other deserts are hot during the day and freezing cold at night.

The Sahara Desert is one of the hottest deserts on Earth. Here, temperatures are scorching hot during the day, but drop below 32° F (0° C) at night. The deserts of North America and the Gobi Desert in Asia are well known for their warm climates. During the winter, however, temperatures can become so cold that the landscape is sometimes dusted with a thin layer of snow.

Expansion

The world's desert ecosystems continually grow and expand. Covered in sand, gravel, or rock, desert landscapes are always changing. Erosion wears away the rock and sand. Flash flooding can move the land.

Eco Facts

Gobi means "waterless place" in Mongolian, one of the languages spoken in China.

Sahara is the Arabic word for "desert" or "deserted land."

Erosion

Erosion is the process of land being worn away by wind, rain, or water. Most deserts are covered in small pebbles or gravel that has broken away from larger stone structures. With no shelter from trees, rock formations are worn away and chipped by wind and rain. These larger pieces of rock break into smaller boulders. Boulders become rocks. Over time, rocks become sand.

Flooding

Flash flooding rarely occurs in deserts. When flash floods do occur, however, the water can cause great movement in the desert landscape. Flash flooding takes place when bursts of water cover large parts of the desert land in just a few minutes. The force of these brief and fast floods carries away loose rocks and sand. There are very few plants or trees to prevent the soil from washing away.

Growth

Sometimes, animals eat all of the vegetation, or plant life, in fertile areas near deserts. These areas are too dry to grow new plants, so they become part of the desert landscape. In this way, deserts constantly grow in size. Wind, rain, mining, and logging also cause deserts to form.

Erosion can cause desert rivers to be diverted along different paths. When this happens, the plants that depended on the river water die.

Types of Deserts

Coastal deserts usually form on the western coasts of continents.

Deserts form for many reasons. Geographic location, climate, precipitation, and elements such as wind influence the creation of desert ecosystems. There are four main types of desert.

Hot Deserts

Giant masses of air swirl above Earth's surface. As Earth rotates, hot air rushes toward the equator. This air moves north and south through the Tropic of Cancer and the Tropic of Capricorn. As the warm air moves nearer to Earth's surface, it absorbs moisture from the air and land. This process dries out the desert landscape.

Rain Shadow Deserts

Rain shadow deserts are found in areas that are sheltered by tall mountain ranges. The ranges block precipitation and ocean moisture from reaching the land. This creates pockets of desert land.

Coastal Deserts

Coastal deserts are located near water. These deserts have hot climates with little rain. Coastal deserts are often covered in mist or fog, but water evaporates too quickly for many types of plants to grow.

Polar Deserts

In the Arctic and Antarctic, there are large areas of rock that are rarely covered in ice and snow. Polar deserts are found in areas with cool temperatures and little precipitation.

Eco Facts

Sometimes, ecosystems are side by side. The Mount Charleston Wilderness area serves as an **oasis** from the surrounding Nevada desert. The recreational area contains 18,000 acres (7,284 hectares) of bristlecone pine that provide a habitat for Rocky Mountain elk.

Desert Features

Deserts are made up of sand, pebbles, rock, or **basalt**. Deserts may look different, but they all have some common physical features.

Playas

Playas are large, flat basins filled with salt or clay. During a flood, basins fill with water that quickly evaporates. Salt or clay rises to the surface of the basins. This salt and clay remain on the surface even after the water disappears.

Plateaus

Plateaus are large areas where the land is almost completely flat. In these areas, there are no trees or rock formations.

Sand Dunes

A sand dune is a hill or ridge created by sand deposits. A sand dune can be smaller than 3 feet (1 meter) high, or taller than 600 feet (183 m). There are five kinds of sand dunes: crescent, dome, linear, parabolic, and star-shaped.

Oases

Oases are island-like areas where the land is green and fertile. Oases form when water is trapped between hard rock, called bedrock, and the sandy or rocky desert floor.

Rock Formations

Wind and rain wear away rock over millions of years, creating rock formations. Rock formations include canyons, rock slabs, boulders, caves, arches, or tall, slim pillars rising up from the land.

High winds in the Sahara Desert near Egypt create rock formations called "mushroom rocks."

13

Life in the Desert

It is difficult for plants and animals to survive in desert ecosystems. Despite extreme temperatures and the lack of food, water, and shelter, deserts are filled with some of the world's most interesting plants and animals. These plants and animals depend on each other for the food, or energy, they need to survive. This energy transfers from one organism to another through the food chain.

Producers

The plants found in deserts act as producers for other organisms in the ecosystem. These organisms are called producers because they make their own food. They also serve as food for other organisms. Producers absorb energy from the Sun and convert it into usable forms of energy such as sugar. They make this energy through a process called **photosynthesis**. Producers found in deserts include cacti and certain types of grasses, shrubs, and trees.

Primary Consumers

The insects and animals that rely on producers as a food source are called primary consumers. When a primary consumer feeds on a producer, the energy made by the producer is transferred to the consumer. Examples of primary consumers found in desert ecosystems include insects and some mammals, such as mice and rats. Reptiles can also be primary consumers. The chuckwalla, a type of iguana, and the desert tortoise are primary consumers.

Rainforest Energy Pyramid

The transfer of energy in an ecosystem begins with producers and moves up the energy pyramid to the tertiary consumers. Organisms at each level of the pyramid receive energy from the organisms in the level below them.

Outside of the pyramid are the decomposers. They break down the dead and decaying organic matter left behind when plants and animals die. For this reason, decomposers receive energy from organisms in all levels of the energy pyramid.

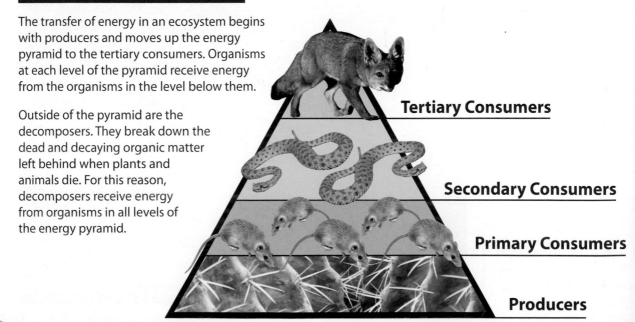

Tertiary Consumers

Secondary Consumers

Primary Consumers

Producers

Desert Food Web

Another way to study the flow of energy through an ecosystem is by examining food chains and food webs. A food chain shows how a producer feeds a primary consumer, which then feeds a secondary consumer, and so on. However, most organisms feed on many different food sources. This practice causes food chains to interconnect, creating a food web.

In this example, the **red line** represents one food chain from the cactus, ants, and hawk. The blue line from the joshua tree, beetle, lizard, and hawk form another food chain. These food chains connect at the owl, but they also connect in other places. The grasshopper also feeds from grass, and the cougar also eats cardinals. This series of connections forms a complex food web.

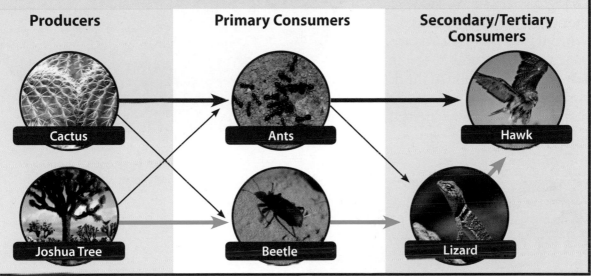

Producers	Primary Consumers	Secondary/Tertiary Consumers
Cactus	Ants	Hawk
Joshua Tree	Beetle	Lizard

Secondary and Tertiary Consumers

Secondary consumers feed on both producers and primary consumers. In the desert, secondary consumers include reptiles and **amphibians**, such as small snakes and frogs. Spiders, most birds, and some mammals, including the mongoose, are also secondary consumers. Larger carnivores, such as foxes, and some large snakes, including rattlesnakes, are called tertiary consumers. Tertiary consumers feed on secondary consumers.

Decomposers

Fungi, such as mushrooms, and many types of bacteria live in desert ecosystems. These organisms are called decomposers because they eat dead and decaying **organic** materials. Decomposers speed up the process of breaking down dead organic materials and releasing their **nutrients** into the soil. These nutrients are then absorbed by the roots of trees and other plants.

Plants

Cacti

Many cacti grow in rocky desert ecosystems. These plants do not have long root structures to help them absorb water. Instead, they act as sponges, storing water in their pith, or tissue. Cacti are pleated like an accordion, so when water is available, they expand. There is little water in the desert, so many cacti grow very slowly. However, they often live for hundreds of years. When the average saguaro cactus is 80 years old, it is only 20 feet (6 m) tall. Other cacti found in the desert are barrel and organ-pipe cacti. They have been named because of the objects they resemble.

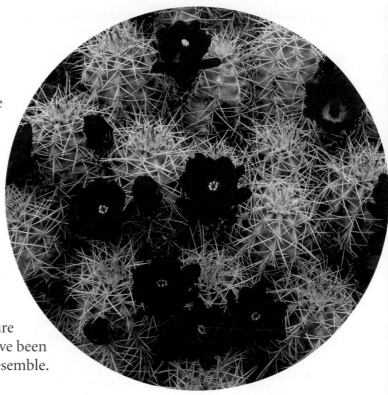

The claret cup cactus produces brightly colored flowers and edible fruit.

Trees

Some of the world's most fascinating trees are found in desert ecosystems. Baobab trees, which grow in the deserts of Africa, have thick, spongy trunks that are used to store water. Joshua trees are covered with spines that make them look hairy. The spines shelter the trees from the hot desert sunshine so they can conserve water. Other trees, such as mesquite trees, have long root systems that draw water from great distances. The roots of a mesquite tree can be 100 feet (30.5 m) long.

Joshua trees grow only in the Mojave Desert. They can be up to 40 feet (12 m) tall.

Eco Facts

Saguaro cacti are made up of about 90 percent water. Saguaro cacti bloom in the spring. For 24 hours, they sprout a beautiful blossom that contains sweet nectar. Desert animals, such as birds and bats, eat this nectar. Saguaro cacti also provide shelter for some desert animals. Birds, including woodpeckers, owls, hawks, and sparrows, nest in the cacti.

Plants and Shrubs

Water escapes through a plant's leaves, so many desert plants and shrubs lose their leaves during times of **drought**. This helps them conserve water. Plants such as the acacia and ocotillo spring to life and grow new leaves when there is rain. Other plants have very short life spans. Seeds from flowering plants, such as the claret cup, wait for rain. When rain falls, they bloom and cover the desert floor in a wash of color. Most only live for one or two days.

The agave of the Sonoran Desert are used to make a sweetener called agave nectar.

Birds and Mammals

Camels

Dromedary and bactrian camels are very common in the world's desert ecosystems. The dromedary has one hump, and the bactrian has two. Camels can drink as much as 53 gallons (200 liters) of water at a time. This helps them stay **hydrated** when water is scarce. Camels have adapted to desert life in other ways, too. Their wide hooves help them to walk on sand very easily without sinking. Camels look like they are floating across the sand when they walk. They are called "ships of the desert" because they have been used to carry people and goods across the desert for hundreds of years.

Bactrian camels have two sets of eyelashes to protect their eyes from sand.

The pygmy falcon of Africa is one of the smallest birds of prey.

Birds

Birds are a common sight in desert ecosystems. Birds can fly long distances to find food and water. Their feathers also help them regulate, or change, their body heat and protect them from the scorching sunshine. Falcons fly above the barren landscape in search of small rodents and lizards to eat. Lanner falcons use their hooked beaks and sharp talons to capture and eat their prey. Tiny elf owls nest in cacti and take shelter from the warm desert sunshine. When the Sun sets each day, these owls, which only grow to be 5 inches (13 cm) tall, hunt for insects and lizards to eat.

Eco Facts

Many animals and birds take shelter underground where it is cooler. Burrowing owls have long legs that they use to dig tunnels and burrows. Egyptian jerboas, a type of rodent, also live in underground homes that protect them from heat and predators.

Mammals

Each desert ecosystem is home to a variety of mammals. These mammals have found many different ways to survive with little water, in extreme temperatures, and with very little to eat. Savanna elephants can be found in the deserts of Africa. They share the area with addaxes, a type of antelope, lions, and hundreds of species of rodents. Other mammals, such as the kangaroo, hop through the dusty Outback of Australia. Kangaroos can jump distances up to 30 feet (9 m) in a single leap. The fennec fox, which only grows to be 16 inches (40 cm) tall, has enormous ears that cool its body. Caracals, a type of wildcat, have very long legs that help them run quickly and jump in the air to catch prey.

African elephants are the largest living land animals.

19

Insects, Amphibians, and Reptiles

The Namib Desert beetle survives in its dry habitat by collecting water from early-morning fog.

Insects

Invertebrates are the smallest desert creatures. They have found unusual ways to battle the treacherous conditions of their habitat. In the Sahara Desert, scorpions are covered with protective plates that act as armor. Their curved tail has a stinger that can poison their prey. Some invertebrates collect water to help them survive. The Namib Desert beetle collects water that condenses, or gathers, on its body. Ants thrive in desert sands, where they build elaborate colonies. When ant lions are **larvae**, they build tunnels that are up to 2 inches (5 cm) deep. The larvae have strong jaws, which they use to eat insects that fall into their traps.

Amphibians

Amphibians depend on water to survive, but some have special adaptations to help them live in dry, desert conditions. Spadefoot toads, which are common in North America, store fat in their bodies to help them survive during periods of drought. The Australian water-holding frog digs itself an underground burrow that fills with water when it rains. These frogs have a special type of skin that allows them to absorb and retain water.

Water-holding frogs store water in their bladders and pockets of skin.

Eco Facts

A young scorpion spends at least the first two weeks of its life on its mother's back.

Adult ant lions look more like dragonflies than ants.

Spadefoot toads are named for their spade-shaped feet, which they use to dig burrows.

Reptiles

Lizards and snakes enjoy the hot desert sunshine because it keeps them warm. Poisonous gila monsters creep and crawl through deserts in search of bird eggs or other lizards to eat. Thorny devils, another type of lizard, use their sharp spines to protect themselves from predators. Rattlesnakes live in the deserts of North and South America. The most common type of rattlesnake is the western diamondback rattlesnake, which gets its name from the diamond-shaped pattern on its skin.

Up to 2 feet (0.6 m) long and weighing as much as 5 pounds (2.3 kilograms), the gila monster is the largest lizard native to the United States.

Deserts in Danger

The harsh conditions in desert ecosystems make it difficult for species to survive. Still, adapting to a lack of shelter, food, and water is not the only challenge desert creatures face. Many desert animals are threatened with extinction because of human development, pollution, and mining. Animals in danger of becoming extinct are classified as endangered. This means that there are so few of the species remaining that they need protection in order to survive. In the United States, it is against the law to hunt or harm endangered animals.

The Arabian oryx is a medium-sized antelope species that lives in the Arabian Desert. These animals have nearly become extinct because humans hunt them for their meat, fur, and horns. Zoos breed the Arabian oryx to help keep the species from dying out completely.

Elephants are also faced with the threat of extinction. Their long ivory tusks make them valuable to hunters, who sell these body parts to people who make jewelry and other items. It is now illegal to hunt elephants.

Mining and development threaten desert habitats. Heavy development and mining in deserts in North and South America, Egypt, and Africa have destroyed many animal habitats.

Timeline of Human Activity in Deserts

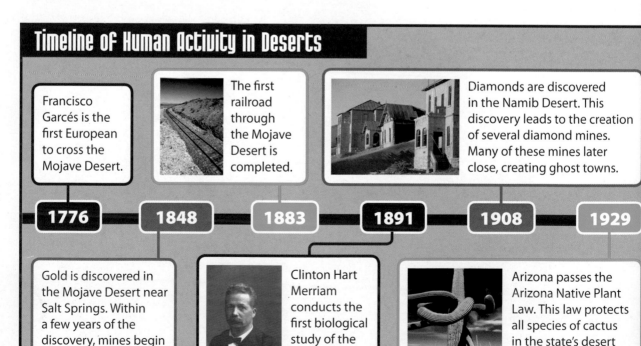

Francisco Garcés is the first European to cross the Mojave Desert.

The first railroad through the Mojave Desert is completed.

Diamonds are discovered in the Namib Desert. This discovery leads to the creation of several diamond mines. Many of these mines later close, creating ghost towns.

1776 — **1848** — **1883** — **1891** — **1908** — **1929**

Gold is discovered in the Mojave Desert near Salt Springs. Within a few years of the discovery, mines begin to operate in the area.

Clinton Hart Merriam conducts the first biological study of the **Death Valley** ecosystem.

Arizona passes the Arizona Native Plant Law. This law protects all species of cactus in the state's desert ecosystems.

Large-scale mining operations threaten the plants and animals that live in desert ecosystems.

A group of scientists meets in Paris, France, to discuss the creation of an international advisory committee for issues affecting desert areas.

An international conference meets in Paris to discuss ways to conserve the resources of the biosphere.

The UN declares this the International Year of Deserts and Desertification.

1949   **1960s**   **1968**   **1994**   **2001**   **2006**

The number of people living in the Mojave Desert begins to rise rapidly.

The United Nations (UN) adopts the Convention to Combat Desertification on June 17. The same day is proclaimed World Day to Combat Desertification.

The U.S. Bureau of Land Management bans off-road vehicle use in 750 square miles (1,940 sq. km) of the Sonoran and Mojave Deserts.

Science in the Desert

Wind turbines are a virtually pollution-free source of renewable energy.

People are always looking for new ways to cope with the desert's harsh conditions. Deserts have a network of water and energy resources that people can use to nourish the land and power buildings. Scientists strive to find new means to learn about and use desert resources. New technologies are continually developed.

Watering the Desert

Although deserts are dry and barren on the surface, many have huge reserves of water below the ground. Others are located near major rivers. People often look for ways to use these sources to **irrigate** the dry desert land. Farmers use irrigation to water crops. Many deserts are rich in the **minerals** and nutrients that crops need to survive. Few people can live in deserts because the conditions are too harsh and water is difficult to find.

Canals

In deserts located near large rivers or lakes, people use canals to irrigate the dry land. Canals are human-made lakes that move water from one source to another. In parts of the Arabian Desert, people dig canals that are connected to wells so that communities can use the water for crops, animals, and personal consumption.

Eco Facts

The largest source of artesian water in the world is found in the Great Artesian Basin in Australia. This basin is made up of three smaller basins. They are the Carpentaria, the Eyre, and the Murray Basins.

Aquifers

Some rocks are porous, which means they absorb water like a sponge. These rocks are called aquifers. Located below some deserts are layers of aquifers that absorb and hold any moisture that falls on desert soil. People dig holes to reach aquifers and bring water to the surface of the land. Artesian water is the name given to the aquifers beneath the ground.

Solar Power

In addition to water, scientists capture heat and energy from the Sun to provide electricity to areas surrounding deserts. This is called solar power. In some deserts, scientists have built hundreds of large, mirrored panels to capture **solar energy**.

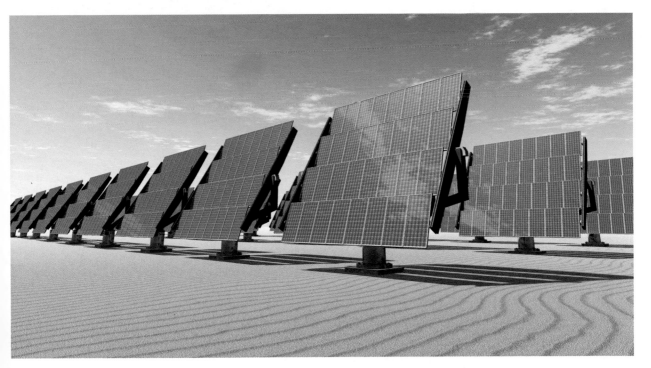

The Mojave Desert is home to several solar energy generating systems (SEGS). The high levels of solar radiation in the Mojave make it an ideal location for SEGS.

Working in the Desert

Scientists who work in desert ecosystems have to be prepared to work in dangerous environments.

People who work in desert ecosystems must have a strong background in science, math, history, and culture. A good education is needed for a range of activities, from studying unique creatures to helping people water their land and protect arid environments. Though there are many types of jobs that involve studying the desert, most people who work in these environments study ecology.

Ecologist

Duties

Studies the relationship between organisms and their habitats as well as actions that affect this relationship

Education

Bachelor of science or masters of ecology degree

Interests

Earth science, ecosystems, geology, biology, climatology, the environment

Ecologists study the plants, animals, and climates of desert ecosystems. They work to protect the living creatures that live in the desert. Ecologists often work with environmental groups to determine what effect a certain action or product might have on the environment.

Other Desert Jobs

Professor of Ecology

Teaches classes about ecology in colleges and universities

Environmental Consultant

Studies how humans interact with deserts and looks for ways to protect ecosystems

Biologist

Studies the plant and animal life found in deserts and anything that affects the natural balance in the ecosystem.

Eugene Pleasants Odum

Eugene Pleasants Odum (1913–2002) is credited with bringing the study of ecology into prominence in mainstream science. Odum earned a bachelor of science degree at the University of North Carolina and later graduated with a doctoral degree from the University of Illinois.

In 1953, he wrote the first major textbook on ecology, *Fundamentals of Ecology*. Odum helped further establish ecology as its own discipline of study when he created the Institute of Ecology at the University of Georgia in 1961. He also led research at the Savannah River Ecology Laboratory, which was one of the largest ecology research centers in the world at the time. There, Odum studied the effects of a nearby nuclear weapons plant on the surrounding environment.

Odum won the Tyler Ecological Award in 1977. This award is given each year to a person who has made outstanding contributions to preserving and enhancing the environment. Odum won numerous awards for his efforts in teaching, including the 1983 National Wildlife Federation Educator of the Year award.

A 2002 study found that members of the American Institute of Biological Sciences considered *Fundamentals of Ecology* the single book that had the greatest impact on their careers in science.

Build a Solar Still

Ｐeople have found many ways to survive in desert ecosystems. For example, people use solar stills to gather water. Try building a solar still in your backyard.

clear garbage bag

a shovel

8 to 10 medium-sized rocks

one smaller rock

a measuring glass

Materials

1 With the help of an adult, dig a round hole in a sandbox or garden. The hole must have a flat bottom and should be no bigger than a garbage bag.

2 Put the measuring glass in the center of the hole.

3 Lay the garbage bag over the top of the hole. Put the medium-sized rocks around the bag to hold it in place.

4 Place the small rock in the center of the bag over the measuring glass, and wait for it to fill with water.

Results

Over time, moisture from the ground and heat from the Sun cause condensation to form on the underside of the bag. The rock in the center of the bag directs the water to run into the measuring glass. Check the measuring glass to find out how much water you collected.

Create a Food Web

Use this book, and research on the Internet, to create a food web of desert ecosystem plants and animals. Start by finding at least three organisms of each type—producers, primary consumers, secondary consumers, and tertiary consumers. Then, begin linking these organisms together into food chains. Draw the arrows of each food chain in a different color. Use a **red** pen or crayon for one food chain and green and blue for the others. You should find that many of these food chains connect, creating a food web. Add the rest of the arrows to complete the food web using a pencil or **black** pen.

Once your food web is complete, use it to answer the following questions.

1 How would removing one organism from your food web affect the other organisms in the web?

2 What would happen to the rest of the food web if the producers were taken away?

3 How would decomposers fit into the food web?

Sample Food Web

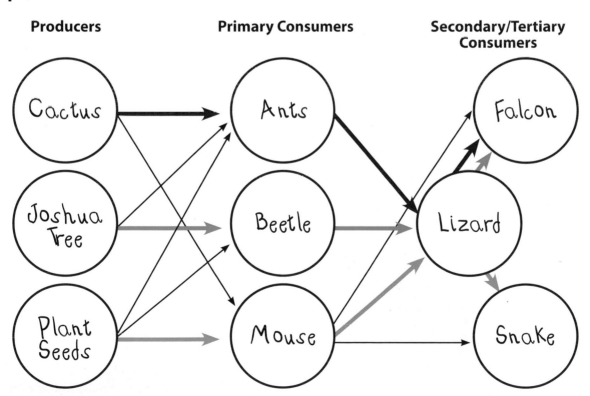

Producers	Primary Consumers	Secondary/Tertiary Consumers
Cactus	Ants	Falcon
Joshua Tree	Beetle	Lizard
Plant Seeds	Mouse	Snake

Eco Challenge

1. How many continents have deserts?

2. What are the four types of deserts?

3. Name five desert features.

4. How high can temperatures reach in a hot desert?

5. Name three desert careers.

6. What type of water is found in aquifers?

7. What special adaptation do camels have?

8. Why do people hunt elephants?

9. Which animals are the desert's smallest creatures?

10. Where do cacti store water?

Glossary

adapted: changed to suit the environment

amphibians: cold-blooded animals with moist, smooth skin

basalt: rock made from volcanic lava

Death Valley: part of the Mojave Desert; features the hottest and driest environment in North America

drought: a period of dry weather

ecosystems: communities of living things sharing an environment

equator: an imaginary line drawn around Earth's center

hydrated: supplied with water to maintain a fluid balance

irrigate: to provide water to dry land through ditches, channels, streams, or pipes

larvae: the young of any invertebrate

minerals: non-organic substances or elements that occur in nature

nutrients: substances that feed plants or animals

oasis: a lush area in a desert ecosystem that is capable of supporting life

organic: materials that come from living things

organisms: living things

photosynthesis: the process in which a green plant uses sunlight to change water and carbon dioxide into food for itself

solar energy: power created using energy from the Sun

species: a group of similar plants and animals that can mate together

Tropic of Cancer: an imaginary line north of the equator

Tropic of Capricorn: an imaginary line south of the equator

Index

Log on to www.av2books.com

AV² by Weigl brings you media enhanced books that support active learning. Go to www.av2books.com, and enter the special code found on page 2 of this book. You will gain access to enriched and enhanced content that supplements and complements this book. Content includes video, audio, web links, quizzes, a slide show, and activities.

Audio
Listen to sections of the book read aloud.

Video
Watch informative video clips.

Embedded Weblinks
Gain additional information for research.

Try This!
Complete activities and hands-on experiments.

WHAT'S ONLINE?

Try This!	Embedded Weblinks	Video	EXTRA FEATURES
Map deserts around the world.	Learn more about deserts.	Watch a video about deserts.	**Audio** Listen to sections of the book read aloud.
Find out more about animals that live in deserts.	Find current weather forecasts in deserts.	Watch a video about an animal that lives in a desert.	
Test your knowledge of human activity in deserts.	Learn how to identify different plants in deserts.		**Key Words** Study vocabulary, and complete a matching word activity.
Write a descriptive paragraph about a day in the life of scientists working in deserts.	Read about current research in deserts.		**Slide Show** View images and captions and prepare a presentation
	Learn more about food chains.		**Quizzes** Test your knowledge.

AV² was built to bridge the gap between print and digital. We encourage you to tell us what you like and what you want to see in the future.

Sign up to be an AV² Ambassador at www.av2books.com/ambassador.